QUEEN'S
DESIRE

SAIRA PRIEST

A Book Poem

COPYRIGHT

QUEEN'S DESIRE
A Book Poem

© 2020 by Saira Priest

ISBN: 978-0-9726628-3-3

all rights reserved
Niche Publishing
NichePublishing.US
sairapriest.com
queensdesirepoem.com

Credits:
Foreword: Angela Myers
Cover Design Assistance: Kelson McLuen
Queen Editor: Gayle Bodine
Blue Crown image: Opensource
Girl Mermaid image: Vectorstock Expanded License
Blue Mandala image: Carole Neale
Iceberg Heart image: included in Apple Pages
Neptune image: NASA/JPL
"Into the Dance" image: Saira Priest

QUEEN'S
DESIRE

SAIRA PRIEST

A Book Poem

FOREWORD

Wow! I am breathless. I want to read this poem many times over. It is simple, eloquent, profound, prophetic, heart-portal-realness.

The journey of Queen's Desire enveloped me in visual after visual and spoke to the inner landscape of what it is to walk this life. I felt like I was witnessing not only myself, but all of humanity and our unfolding.

Beginning with the two-directional arrow - inward and outward - released from the bow of a question, our intent to Know, we initiate the cascade of our full becoming.

In our world of action, all things must happen. And still, through the doorways of consciousness pulsates the unyielding impetus of our sacred journey Home.

We cringe, cry, and create inside the swinging dualities housed in SpaceTime - the epic adventure of Divine Soul and our wrestling with the paradoxes - that combined answer to the whole of our Being-ness.

The billion-year revolution of co-creative evolution - we must experience the full pilgrimage so we can land right where we began: in our very own Heart.

Queen's Desire is:

a Tale of the Times,
a Cosmic Her-story,
Human. Quantum. Molecular.
The Breath of the Cosmos,
the Queen of Creation,
Desire and all it signifies in a human experience.
Us looking for Us,
tearing it apart to remember it is not separate.

Losing the Way, Finding Home, Destiny, Choice, Struggle, our Illusions and Dreams, the Veil... encapsulating the core of our Truth as humanity, the Divine Feminine, Earth, Cosmos, the continual ebb and flow of existence, the Great Play, the shattering and the repairing, the ecstasy and the horror... sonorous phrases grace the pages:

Singularity of Circularity,
expanding game of chess,
The Golden Age of Planetary Missions!

This is the sacred honor of being on Earth - our connected existence enriches and co-creates the Cosmic fabric. This is the ancient tale woven into the silk fabric of Queen's Desire.

I am inspired. I humbly bow to these words. I send gratitude for the being who wrote/channeled/ loved these words into being. For the one to put these words into form can only be one of great depth, sensitivity, honesty, and fearlessness.

I am so touched by the gentle way Queen's Desire lands me back into the Center of my Being, into my core, to Remember mySelf, to hold hands with Goddess/He/She because we are already United, and we progress on this pilgrimage because it is simply there for the benefit of All That Is.

Queen's Desire helps us remember that our journey is simply for the good of it, in and of itself, for we are already WHOLE! A redemptive and gorgeous, forgiving, gently spiraling tale.

There can be no better time for the truth of this poem
to gift its grace into the world.
The time for this work's medicine is now,
exactly now.

By Angela Myers
Co-Author of "Spirit"

INTRODUCTION

From the Author

How Queen's Desire Came to Be.
During the many years of writing and researching for my upcoming novel, I wondered what power women have had throughout time to affect change in our environment.

At an intensive retreat with like-minded seekers, my new friends cheered me on to finalize this coming-of-age story.

I returned home, eager to complete that work. However, instead of birthing the novel, this poem came rushing through.

Unaware that it was going to be so long, I jotted it down in a notebook from back to front, overlapping some other written items. The poem flowed like a waterfall over days.

Soon, I realized that it needed to be typed, because I would never be able to decipher the hurried sequence if I waited to do it in the future. And so was born this book length poem. It is a culmination of studies of the Silk Road and spiritual lessons learned along the way. As I was reworking the poem for timelessness, a modern-day-duchess dilemma unfolded, of which you may find some hint.

After months of mustering up courage, I sent the poem to a fellow writer and friend for feedback. With deep resonance and reflection, Angela the poetess nurtured me to bring Queen's Desire out into the world.

With guidance from many other kind souls and deep gratitude in my heart, I am now able to share Her with you.

QUEEN'S DESIRE

TABLE OF CONTENTS

Foreword

Introduction

    Opening   1

    The Qualm of the Queen's Desire   8

    The Quagmire of the Queen's Desire   17

    The Quintessence of the Queen's Desire   42

    Epilogue   63

Gratitude

A Word to the Reader

Other Works

Follow the Author

OPENING

QUEEN'S DESIRE

What springs forth from the
Desire of a Queen?

"I want some," said She
Thus began a prophecy . . .

Which flowers
chosen to bloom
Which jewels festooned
the groom

Which carpets shall
grace the floor
Which tastes fill table and
hand-picked guests,
begging for more

Which artisans prize-possessed
Which dancers danced
Created from questions only
She hath chanced

QUEEN'S DESIRE

What cloth and textile
shall be woven
Which shall be the revered:
shaman or coven

What shall define
our beauty,
which behaviors
delineate duty

What colors will wave
on tents, body, air
Which goods stocked
in souks offering fare

What laws shall govern
the land, its peoples
What children bear
the scars of
unfulfilled desires
of the Queen

Because of some
offense, or touch of hand,
which wars were waged
and prisoners caged
on Her demand
in acts of rage

Which innovations,
technologies emerged
which Her desire urged

Which jewels unearthed
and which rocks quarried
Whose was what,
when who,
with whom,
was married

Which hearts were mended
which hearts torn asunder
from Her loving light, or
Her fire and Her thunder

Which gardens
did She grow
as She gently tended
When kindnesses
were spoken
or in shame
When all was curried
in the name of fame

Which treasuries and stories
yet remain in mystery
For this we have the gift of
evolving history

Let's thank
the observer, the scribe,
the librarian, the keeper,
Precious preserver
of the house of wisdom,
Ignorance curer!

As truths are truths
ever-emerging
Ever-evolving,
as well
is our humanity
Up the spiral
and through the fractal, we yearn
Evolution
urges us to grow, to learn

So in truth,
we grow ever smarter
in seeking out
                . . . our *Star Starter*!

The Qualm of the
QUEEN'S DESIRE

QUEEN'S DESIRE

Questions of Queens
are created
in company
In collaboration
by community

When stripped of fairytale
Freed
from some facility held
seeking sanctuary
- a sovereignty
of Her own mind-making:

The dream . . .
    of being Queen . . .
        Someday . . .
Pampered and beautiful
of luxury and of leisure,
The paradise She seeks
may be the now
which She is living . . .

The paradox and the promise
of the tiara and the title
The rule of the castle
To be named Monarch,
Hailed, Her Majesty

When subsides the attention
and the glory . . .

Awareness dawns the reality,
the sheerness of responsibility
The commitments of consistency
for a lifetime, not to be taken lightly

All in order and in efficiency
Traditions to uphold
Heredity
A code of fixed pageantry
The great request of royalty

Where Her presence is
mandatory and Her time
no longer Her own
Her public demands their Queen
Dressed up and looking supreme

Poised and prepared
Proclaimed for all to admire
Elegant and dignified
Modeling to inspire
Her every moment and move
Practiced with grace
sit up straight
hair in place
made up face

Strict must be Her calendar
Of obligation
Appearance
Expectation
of Perfection
Announcements
Pronouncements
Declarations
and Decrees

Parades,
Balls and dances
merry and lively
In palaces full of
Pedigrees

With different freedoms
another enclosure
is opened for Her
of discipline and of manner

Every day a new directive
more to do and more to give

Earnest eyes,
    inquisitive
    stern
    and discriminative

                What does She wear
What does She eat
How much,
       When and Where

What does She fancy

What does She say?

Careful
words
to
be
chosen

Precise language
in each
one
Conveying
clear meaning
Only
can be spoken

In quandary
and in qualm
Her voice
they need
to hear to calm

Panics to quell,
prevent anarchy
To peace,
She holds the key. . .

When caught up
in the frenzy,
flurry
of activity . . .

STOP

S l o w d o w n...

to do

Nothing

momentarily,
also an option be.

Now, She seeks
another kind of free
Spirit aligns
Sweetly surrenders, She,
a vessel for Divine
Love becomes
and lives in freedom,
nowhere else found . . .

"*This* is *Life!*"
... a whisper comes

The Quagmire of the
QUEEN'S DESIRE

QUEEN'S DESIRE

Out of a Queen's Desire
        flow many things…

Gems and stones and golden rings
Scarves and flags, for all the best
Miles traveled in hundreds
Pearls from oceans deep

Mountains climbed, deserts crossed -
for every Queen, a thousand journeys made,
Goblets of silver, mirrors gem-studded

Which spices tantalized Her tastes
In conquest, countries,
islands laid to waste

Which stories spread
far and wide,
To which heights' ascent
Her heart's desire to satisfy
Now fig, now date, now scent

Creatures dead
for bone and plume
Forests felled
for extra room
to store Her hoards
yet wanting more

Hands marred and faces encrusted,
bodies hanged and resurrected
for idol and for obelisk,
strands of saffron,
cocoons of silk

For Her crown, blue diamonds
For Her gowns, fine satin
Her drink in glass, Venetian
Kohl for eyes exotic

The miracles, the magic
The days of peace
and the blood of war
from Her simple pick

Which cities crumble
and churches fire
and every crisis
births an empire
- Newer!

As babies grow
in women's wombs
worlds by Queens
are birthed too

Planets and the Universe
as all shall one day rest in tombs
Just think of all the Queens of time
and Oh! the galaxies they grew!

Who is this Queen
such authority hath
She runs through all
from that first
primordial breath

Wonder *The Thought!*
 that formed this world
 and pulses
 through us all,
 The Evolutionary Urge

What Sound!
 What Breath!
  that blew the
   dust of stars
    forever outward . . .

In it,
through it,
Arrived
the singularity
of Her,
of You!

Imagine!
. . . the strength of
that same breath
in you . . .

. . . *is you*

A lover's whisper,
a baby's squeal
A wolf, a wail, the song of whales
Sweet ancient melody

Through what
Grand Master Symphony
does it orchestrate
The Grand Master Designer,
which? - Apprentice or Architect

What figurine as effigy,
enshrined for legacy
Which mausoleum
or house of worship
still stand erect

For centuries of folk and masters
to admire, marvel
genuflect

What grandiose vision
to faithfully fashion
mosque cerulean
golden palace,
marble mansion

How great the Love
of admirers be
in memorial to
guard for eternity

What relics, indulgences
Sins to absolve
in numbers vary and many

What lengths of ship
and dhow constructed
and in hundreds ferry
The name of some beloved
Queen carry

For whom erected,
statue cast in bronze
uncontainable
in flesh too small

Driving those around them,
garnered,
on whatever course
multitudes
partnered

Footpaths, roads and crossings
ditches, canals and waterfalls

No force too great
to harness
no resource too far
too deep
too high
too dangerous
to dig

QUEEN'S DESIRE

Mined
in parts and sections
Splitting
and great-walling off nations
Directed
by mis-education
Ignorant
of systems of nature
The whole being
the greater!

The Earth She holds
so many treasures
Must the Queen
own all of this
Are they not already Hers
where they exist?

What once She coveted
She now abhors
Her every desire stuffed
in countless parlors
Yet still She yens, She craves

To consume world wealth,
how many loves disrupted,
diseases contracted

Which coins were cut
and steels forged
While at Her castle,
the Queen gorged

How many untold lives
Sweetened Her fate
For ambrosial hunger
to satiate

Choice-less,
oblige them She,
save free will,
Their's, in *Her* destiny

Which child excelled
beyond compare
Which crowds compelled
to stop and stare

In works of horror
or goodness gleaned
Rumors spoken
through wine
as others cleaned

Plays on stages enacted
of lives shattered and healed
Glimpsing stolen wives
in theaters acted
Who watched in rags
Who, in silken tapestry

Who juggled and
who clowned around,
Tigers or elephants
traveling to town

In jubilees and jamborees
Celebrations and ceremonies
galore
Confetti, petals cover
the floor

Bands of music
singing praise
All form of riches
are appraised

Packages wrapped
in elegance
Fanfare, pomp
and circumstance
Her deep desire to fill

Kingdoms on campaigns
to courts imperial
for grasses greener
What weight of riches
on backs of camels,
horses, slaves, growing leaner

Which religions shared by
mouth and word
Scents and styles and sounds
once never heard

QUEEN'S DESIRE

How many missions made,
hajj's and crusades,
The catalyst of a chain reaction
spread plagues,
and ages of illumination

How many lifetimes
spent astrolabe inventing
better instruments of peace
and war preventing

Out of desire born
philosophies torn
Is struggle real
or necessary
Is desire our birthright
or adversary

The secret of life
the fountain of youth
the holy grail

Which is dream,
which is veil
which is truth
which for sale

A society rises
while one falls,
another in ruins
What lessons
do we recall?

Herstory tells tall tales
in events
She weaves
Concurrently run through,
truths hard achieved

Every civilization
which has ever fallen
has had one
thing in common:
the sin of wanting more
-In excess- and no less

To trust the faith
in this constancy
Remember what must be
Bless what is to be set free

The quest to know
it, too, did grow
The drive, the impulse
it, too, greater grew
in some, so rare and few

Are we at the center
of All That Is
or…do we need
All That Is to live -
We, at *Her mercy*?

Making the unknown knowable
while expanding the answers multi-
to make space for each one's
deeper mystery

Tiring of possessions ephemeral
The Queen She asks
questions existential:

> "*Who* am I and
>   Who is my maker?"
>
> "*What*'s my purpose?"
>
> "*Where*'s my place?"
>
> "*When* will I find true love - my soulmate?"
>
> "*How* can I know the date?"

Thus beginning inquiry
Astronomy and astrology
Sciences forming
Droves of students dorming
Fields of fertility

At times,
She ponders
on material plane:

"What is good?"
"What is novel?"
"What is new?"

"What goes on elsewhere?"
"How do they do?"

"Which is beauty?"
"Where is truth?"

"What is possible?"

"What will *you* do?"

Her questions form
eternal quests
of kings, princes,
paupers, guests

Which drove the masses
off their asses
Inspiring questions
of their own

Tortured souls
traversed
on long adventures
for their ailments
seeking cures

Which tales are scripted,
which lost in time
Which battles
were fought
in season
and which
thwarted
by act of mood
or reason
or beloveds courted

Which alliances
by marriages bonded
Which enemies made friends
by how each responded

In time of need
and great despair
Which helping hand,
relationship repaired

Which circles of
Sacred Sisterhood
formed from the bad
and the good

Grounding clans, tribes
Making plans, brides,
soothing fears
which arose,
building bridges,
silk roads

Which heads did roll
when necks did meet
the guillotine
through heartbreak or betrayal

- In Her despair

Which bodies spared
and necks adorned
with medal-ware
through healing and compassion

                              - In Her delight

When She did suppress
the hells to which
there is no compare

Back and forth,
teeter totter, She
Yin and Yang,
Black and White
Coffee, Tea

Soon She finds her bearings
Swaying in practice
to center Her steerings

Then steady on
She goes -
till far to one side
She is thrown

Then swing She does
for momentum's sake
lest all She built
fall into the lake

Back and forth
the pendulum swings -
Until one day the final toll rings

If this be *Her* destiny
then, choice-less, too
may *She* be

Playing out a drama
in some ways eternal
Until We reach
that nirvana portal,

Is it fantasy?
Merging with the
Beloved, One True
Residing forever more
in Ecstasy.

Then there
She stands
at levels unknown
to see if She
can cast Her crown

Trade it in
for a pair of wings
and serve this time
as guides
unseen

QUEEN'S DESIRE

Whispering lessons
of Her years in
training
Knowing how tough
and soft and fun
it had all been

Delighting lightly in
a new role
An epic adventure
of Her Divine Soul!

Where does it reside -
in body or mind,
or in some ether
Can we catch it,
on some tether

What is its Creator
the Source of its Spark -
can we seek it
in the dark?

The Quintessence of the

QUEEN'S DESIRE

QUEEN'S DESIRE

And now, My Friend,
perhaps you want
this Queen's theory of everything:

of God, of eternity,
of creation,
the Big Bang
and the Great Mystery

I'm just like You,
open to musings
on the Secret of Life
and what I find most amusing
is our God -
He may very well also be a *She*
in all Her complexity

Born of desire, creativity
both masculine and with femininity
A Oneness merged in Universality,
A Union born in synergy

Questions swirled inside my head
Research done, raised folks from dead
Living on pages, papyrus, digital
Just trying to understand it all.

Does it have to be hard
A consuming fire
free will? kismet?
What is my heart's true desire?

Answers sought
in books of wise
Parting truths of ease from lies

Symbols and words
written on every surface
Ink squeezed from
every crevice

For the lure of azure
crimson, carmine,
purple pure

Ancient scrolls
copied in number
Saving opals
for all to remember

Scores of scribes
in daily labor
Recording stills
through turning doors

Holding tightly
to passing winds
Keeping wisdoms
from disappearing

Seeing far into the future
Desiring what's true, what's clear

Seeking sapphires
from all the rubble
Wondering why
all the trouble

All the struggle
and the strife
Is it really necessary in this life?

Is ignorance bliss
or knowledge power
Live in a hut
or better in a tower?

Hell or Heaven
Evil and good
Dark and light
What is really
understood?

Desire bears
the weight of choice -
with every choice
a consequence
from decadence
to morality
whom to hurt, whom to save

A Queen
resides
in every home
be it castle,
tent, yurt or cave

Your way, they say,
begins   on the other side.

Hold your judgements,
before you chide
The Law of Karma,
please abide

In some cabin
hideaway
or on streets of main

Oh You, Queen!
of smaller domain
or greatest lair

QUEEN'S DESIRE

Place Heart in Choice
with deepest
Love and Care
Seek a balance -
Lean left or right,
for things to sway

For place in stay,
for stability:
Choose the *middle* way.

In guiding
Desire's aftermath
Peace may we quantify
when counting the stats:
- negativity subtracts,
+ joy and harmony add,
x multiplies, tranquility,
   Love exponentially
in Sacred Geometry
         -find proof!

So where does
bliss reside, She asks

Is She happy as One
or in the many
Should She marry
or be maid
Is suffering not
hand-made?

Flow like water or
grab the reigns
Find the pleasure
in the pains
Tears of joy
Girl or boy

Linear time or
circular
Astral projection
or states of dream -
Is it really
as it seems?

In the space of Nothing,
In the Everything
In states of flow

In the ones and zeros
In the should I stay
or should I go
For if you don't or if you do
eventually, choose, must you
else it be decided for you

Every time you turn the dial . . .
you open a path, one more mile . . .

round and round,
on and on,
through and through
loop-de-loop,
make a decision
where She goes
everybody says,
nobody knows!

Dare we escape
the cycles of Samsara
Lest we fear the
void of forever

Or can we glad with uncertainty
Play, dance and revel
Until it chances upon
our destiny

Perhaps, there is
no product in the process
just an expanding
game of chess

Have we arrived
at any conclusion?
Which is reality
Is non-duality a Unity -
Time being
the greatest illusion

In every era
it does occur
A question drives
What great cause
shall we honor?
A humanity collective,
do most concur

So Here we have our Unity,
for how long shall that be?
Have we returned back
to that
Singularity of Circularity?

We stand always
at the precipice
of learning,
growing evermore
Answering
what is good
and what is bad

What is necessary
what really matters
what is false,
what is fact

We had to learn
what is edible,
what is rot
what is medicine,
what is poison
which herbs help
what food sustains
what cures the ache
which roots cause dreams
shaman dare partake

Lessons upon lessons
building on each other
Teaching one and
all together
A higher calling to serve

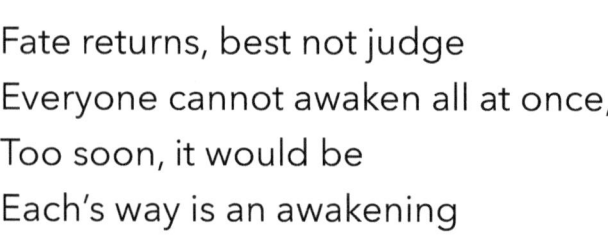

Fate returns, best not judge
Everyone cannot awaken all at once,
Too soon, it would be
Each's way is an awakening
a new day dawning.

She, on the very edge
Evolution Evolving,
evermore
Wiser, stronger
at times, in leaps!

Ushering in a New Era
Nothing less than global:
The Golden Age
of Planetary Missions

Join the revolution of
billions of years of evolution
Take the helm with consciousness
In Co-Creation
with God, hold hands

Luxurious in scope
a new Atlantis,
Universal,
Quantum Jumping thru
heliotropes

Tales are spun
and stories old
pandora boxes,
chests of gold
Phoenixes risings
legends are told
when through dark valleys,
Her imagination grew

Upon reflection
Her light awakened
Of Paradise, Utopia
descriptives too few
to capture the
Magnificence
She once knew

Elysian Fields,
A Garden of Eden,
Shangri-La
A Heaven on Earth
Lead us to
Valhalla
Who will be our savior

A memory distant,
a vision close,
to feel and touch
and savor
granted by Her favor.

Of Her question
esoteric
and abstract,
answers in response,
migrated back . . .

What *is* possible is this:

By energy raised
in groupings
of pulsations
in frequencies higher

Vibration rising
the whole,
- uplifting
A Reset!

A revolution
A leap in evolution
Refreshment

Rejuvenation
Transformation
Restoration

A resurgence
A renewal

A Renaissance!

Where flowers bloom and children play
Such forest lush and fauna grown
Richness in multitudes on display,
These places, we all have known

At long last, sunsets,
and end of days

The final terrain where
every ache is filled
is a return to home,
A return to the Love
we *always* already had -
no greater gold resides
 on any galaxy

Until then, roll along
onward on your pilgrimage
live your personal legacy
quest on
revel in your unique wild ride

Find your center
in a constant state of bliss
on an ever-changing earth

Which rests in time, too,
In all of Eternity
with God in Oneness,
wholeness, in Unity.

Awaken! Oh Queen!
To the truth
of your own creation

Who sees
Your presence
upon this earth
Behold! The Great Omnipresence!

Blesses each experience
Graces you with specific gifts,
Praises all your precious worth
By simply Being,
You have shared since birth.

QUEEN'S DESIRE

For Ultimate Bliss,

My Queen,

is in
Your alignment
with the
Bigger Hands and Heart

of He or She
Who or That
which created Thee

Earned well . . .

Richer . . .

by the Journey.

EPILOGUE

QUEEN'S DESIRE

So now,

Oh, Queen!
 of daily aristocracy,
Shine light on your own legacy
Your life you own,
treat with delicacy

With tender care,
Heal your soul,
With Love for self
You are whole

Be fierce, be kind
learn which to be in time
Reach for the sun
be centered, ground

Direct your desire
Set your intention
Pursue pure passion
Seek, your purpose, be found

QUEEN'S DESIRE

In your seeking
outside-in,
Follow that dream
Return inside and see:
You are already Queen

Commit to The Desire:
Align with Higher Power
Rejoice, laugh, sing,
  and dance The Dance
  with
Exuberance!

QUEEN'S DESIRE

GRATITUDE

So many good hearts helped bring Queen's Desire into being.

Always, I bow first with deepest gratitude to the Divine for the grace granted in my life. Daily, I am blessed.

Next, comes gratitude for my family, every single member. Your support of my work, belief in me, provisions of food, coming through at just the right time, and in all the ways which I may never know. Thank you with my heart full of special love for each of you.

I give thanks to Angela Myers for opening your reflective heart to exchange poetry with me, for the nurturance of this work, for trust in its readiness, for resonance. Deep Gratitude for the Foreword.

To Gayle Bodine, my fellow Floral Card Maker and Reader, I am grateful for the hours of wise woman guidance and cultivation in the rules of creativity.

For My Dear Sister, My Rock. Only Love.

For suggestions on my work and growth as a mentor, many thanks to my intern Kelson McLuen.

To all the seen and un-seen assistance I will continue to receive after this writing, thank you.

Family and Friends, I love and appreciate you all.

QUEEN'S DESIRE

A WORD TO THE READER

To You,
Dear Reader,
A word from the author:

I wish to extend my heartfelt appreciation to you for making the time to read my work.

Your support means so much to me as an indie author, and to the nature loving organizations to which I donate.

THANK YOU!

If you would like to hear a reading of this poem by the author, or other works, as they become available, please sign up at:
www.sairapriest.com
or
www.queensdesirepoem.com.

OTHER WORKS

**Books and Cards
by Saira Priest:**

Coming Soon:

Writing Organically:
A naturally mindful approach for growing your novel

SPIRIT:
Co-authored with Angela Myers

Available Now:

Zen of Hoarding:
108 offerings for deciding what you own

Seek Joy, Find Beauty, Share Love

Floressence Cards

FOLLOW THE AUTHOR

Find Me on:

twitter: @sairapriest
instagram: @queensdesire
            @floressence_cards
            @ageoftherisingfeminine

Reviews
Gladly Accepted
on:

Goodreads
LibraryThing
Amazon
Barnes & Noble
Apple Books

sairapriest.com
queensdesirepoem.com

www.ingramcontent.com/pod-product-compliance
Lightning Source LLC
Chambersburg PA
CBHW042310150426
43198CB00006B/111